COMMITTED
TO ISLAM

A MUSLIM COMMUNITY

SYLVIA AND BARRY
SUTCLIFFE

RMEP

RELIGIOUS AND MORAL EDUCATION PRESS

Religious and Moral Education Press
An imprint of Chansitor Publications Ltd,
a wholly owned subsidiary of Hymns Ancient & Modern Ltd
St Mary's Works, St Mary's Plain
Norwich, Norfolk NR3 3BH

First published 1995

ISBN 1-85175-026-6

Acknowledgements
The Authors and Publisher would like to thank the
Sparkbrook Islamic Centre and the Muslim people it serves,
particularly those whose interviews appear in this book,
for their generous help. We are especially indebted to
Mr Muhammad Afzal, the Centre's Manager, for his kind
assistance as our principal contact in Sparkbrook.

We are also grateful to Articles of Faith, Bury, Lancashire,
and to Exsports, Exeter, for the loan of several items
used in photography.

Designed and typeset by Topics Visual Information, Exeter

Photography by Michael Burton-Pye

Printed in Singapore by Tien Wah Press for
Chansitor Publications Ltd, Norwich

CONTENTS

INTRODUCTION

The books in this **Faith and Commitment** series give you the chance to look at religions and religious denominations (groups within religions) through the personal reflections of people with a religious commitment.

To create these books, we visited local religious communities in different parts of Britain. We talked to people across the range of ages and roles you'd expect to find in a community – parent, child, grandparent, priest, community worker. That is, we interviewed people like you and your family, your friends, the people where you live. We asked them all the same questions and we've used the themes of those questions as chapter headings in the books.

Each chapter contains extracts from those interviews. People interpret our questions as they want to. They talk freely in their own words about religious ideas and personal experiences, putting emphasis where they think it belongs for them. The result is a set of very individual insights into what religion means to some of the people who practise it. A lot of the insights are spiritual ones, so you may have had similar thoughts and experiences yourself, whether or not you consider yourself a 'religious' person.

You will see that some pages include FACT-FINDER boxes. These are linked to what people say in the interview extracts on these pages. They give you bits of back-up information, such as a definition or where to look up a reference to a prayer or a piece of scripture. Remember that these books are not textbooks. We expect you to do some research of your own when you need to. There are plenty of sources to go to and your teacher will be able to help.

There are also photographs all through the books. Some of the items you can see belong to the people whose interview extracts appear on those pages. Most of these items have personal significance. Some have religious or cultural significance, too. They are very special to the people who lent them for particular but different reasons, like special things belonging to you.

Committed to Islam: A Muslim Community introduces you to seven Muslims who use the Sparkbrook Islamic Centre in Birmingham. The Centre has a mosque and is also involved in educational, community and welfare activities on behalf of Muslims in the Sparkbrook area. Many belong to families originally from Pakistan, Bangladesh and Yemen, countries where most Muslims belong to the Sunni sect of Islam.

SYLVIA AND BARRY SUTCLIFFE

ABOUT ME

NAME: *Ifzal A*

WHAT I DO: *I'm in my second year of studying for A-levels at a college about eight miles from here. The A-levels are in Sociology, Law and Business Studies. I hope to go to either Bristol or Nottingham University to read Law. The cricketing facilities at Nottingham are good!*

At college, most of my friends are white, some are Christians. They respect my views and I respect theirs. We've got a good rapport between us. We have an Islamic Society at college. It's open to Muslims and non-Muslims. Every fortnight we have a question-and-answer panel. There's a panel of Muslims and a panel of Christians, and we answer each other's questions. We share our opinions on each other's religion.

MY FAMILY: *I was born in Birmingham. I've got two brothers and two sisters, all younger than me.*

MY ROLE IN THE RELIGIOUS COMMUNITY: *I've been studying at Sparkbrook Islamic Centre for the last thirteen years. It's been a long time. Everything, basically, that I know about the Qur'an and Islam and Urdu I've learned there. I started primary school about the same time as I started studying at the Islamic school. I'd go to the Islamic school every evening from Monday to Friday for about two and a half hours, from five to half-past seven. It seems a lot, but I thought it was all right.*

SOME OF MY SPECIAL INTERESTS: *I'm a keen cricketer. I captain the college and play for a club in the Birmingham League. I open the bowling for its Second XI. I must admit, I've had a pretty successful season. In nineteen matches I've taken forty-seven wickets. I'm the youngest bowler to have done that.*

FACT-FINDER

Qur'an
Islam's sacred book revealed by Allah to the Prophet Muhammad (Peace be upon him).

Urdu
Main language spoken in Pakistan.

NAME: *Nazir A*

MY FAMILY: *I was born and bred in Pakistan. Both my parents are in Pakistan. I've got five children: three boys, two girls. I'm Ifzal's mother.*

MY ROLE IN THE RELIGIOUS COMMUNITY: *I go to the mosque at Sparkbrook Islamic Centre. We have a women's group there and we study the Qur'an together. But mostly I pray at home. When the children are at home, they pray with me. They also go to the mosque. We don't have a special room at home that we use for prayers, but we do make proper preparations. We have prayer-mats, for example.*

SOME OF MY SPECIAL INTERESTS: *I don't really have time for interests. Most of my time is devoted to my family. But I'm happy. I have a good family.*

FACT-FINDER

Qur'an
Islam's sacred book revealed by Allah to the Prophet Muhammad (Peace be upon him).

Prayer-mats
Because prayer performed properly is important in Islam, there are many rules about prayer and preparing to pray. For example, Muslims should pray in a clean place. If they cannot pray in a mosque, they will often use a prayer-mat to make another place suitable.

NAME: *Ibrar K*

WHAT I DO: *I'm originally from Pakistan. I came to Britain in 1969 with my parents, to Bradford. My father worked in the cotton-mills there. He came over in 1961 on his own, then went back to Pakistan for his family in 1968.*

We lived in Bradford for about five years, but the mills were starting to close down. So my father got another job in Birmingham, and I've lived here ever since.

I did my secondary education in Birmingham. When I left school, my father got me my first job in the firm where he worked, but I wasn't happy there. I was more interested in electronics and telecommunications, really. So I applied for and got a job in the telecommunications industry, and I've stayed in it ever since. I've gone to study for specialist qualifications in telecommunications.

MY FAMILY: *I got married ten years ago in Pakistan and brought my wife back with me. We've got four children, all primary-school age.*

MY ROLE IN THE RELIGIOUS COMMUNITY: *I've been involved with the Sparkbrook Islamic Centre since I was a child. I used to go there to study the Qur'an and Arabic. Although the Centre has moved since then I still go to it. There's a mosque attached to it. Some of the other people who go there I've known for years. It's good to meet with them.*

There are other prayer-houses and mosques in the area now, all quite near one another. They all hold five prayer sessions a day, and they stagger the starting-times between them by five or ten minutes or so. This means that if you miss prayers at one mosque you can go to prayers at the next. It gives you a better chance of praying with a congregation, which is really the point of going to a mosque. I mean, we can say our prayers at home, but there's more reward in saying them with a congregation.

FACT-FINDER

Qur'an
Islam's sacred book revealed by Allah to the Prophet Muhammad (Peace be upon him). The Angel Jibril (Gabriel) gave the Prophet the words of the Qur'an in Arabic. (See also page 38.)

NAME: *Farzana K*

MY FAMILY: *I came to Britain from Pakistan ten years ago with my husband Ibrar. Ibrar's maternal grandmother and my maternal grandmother were sisters. If you go back about a hundred years, the two families were quite closely related. That's how they originally got to know each other. In Pakistan, my family lives in a town and Ibrar's family lives in a village.*

When we first got married, Ibrar and I lived with Ibrar's parents not far away from here. Inside the house, it was an environment quite like Pakistan. Ibrar's brother was living there too. He was married with one daughter then. We all used to live like one community within the house. It's a big house with about six bedrooms. It was like a small village in itself.

We moved to our own house about four years ago. That made life more difficult for me. I didn't like it. I wasn't used to living alone. The children would go to school, Ibrar would go to work and I'd be left on my own. What I'd sometimes do was go to Ibrar's parents' house during the day and come back after I'd collected the kids from school.

NAME: *Muhammad Afzal*

MY FAMILY: *I was born in Pakistan, did an MA degree at Karachi University, then came to this country in November 1973. I came on my own. My family joined me in 1977.*

I have four children, all boys. The eldest is in his third year at Cardiff University Medical School. Two are in secondary school, one in Year 10, the other in Year 9. The youngest is in junior school. He's in Year 6.

WHAT I DO

For the first couple of years here I worked with the Muslim Educational Trust, a national organization which is still very active in the education and welfare of Muslim children in Britain.

I've been working at the Sparkbrook Islamic Centre since 1983. My job is Youth and Community Worker, responsible for youth activities, community activities and education as well. I'm also Manager of the Centre at the moment. Most of the people who live and work in this area are Muslim, so it's a large community. About five hundred families are served by the Centre.

There are two main sects in Islam: Shi'ah and Sunni Muslims. Most Muslims, almost ninety per cent in the world, are Sunni, and that's what we are in this community. Shi'ah Muslims are found mostly in Iran and Iraq. Also, in Pakistan there is a large Shi'ah community. But as Sunni Muslims we belong to the main sect of Islam.

I work five days a week at the Sparkbrook Islamic Centre, but I live in Walsall. The place where I live is attached to a mosque which is part of the UK Islamic Mission, so I'm busy at weekends as well. The UK Islamic Mission runs mosques and community activities all over the country, with centres in places like Birmingham, London, Manchester, Bradford, Glasgow, Cardiff and other major cities. I'm Chairman of the Education Committee of the UK Islamic Mission. We run evening schools, devise syllabuses and exams, hold things like speech competitions for boys and girls.

There are quite a lot of trophies on the wall behind me. These have been won by children here at Sparkbrook Islamic Centre. There are twenty-two centres like this one around the country and we teach four subjects: Qur'an Reading, Qur'an Memorization, Islamic Studies and Urdu. Every year there are exams and competitions for the children. The centre which comes first gets a shield. We're quite successful here.

The children who come here – and some have been coming since the age of five – are making a commitment. They have main school during the day, then they come here every evening, about three hundred of them. A big activity of this Centre is hosting visits from non-Muslims. A question that is continually being asked by visitors is how do we get so many children to attend the evening school.

As Muslims, we think it is very, very important that our children learn about their faith, their culture and their roots. Of course, children will be children. If they're not coming to mosque, they're not likely to be tucked up in their beds, either. They could be out wandering the streets or watching the television. We believe that what we're offering them in evening school is something positive. If children are brought up as good Muslims, they will go on to be good citizens of this country. Islam teaches them respect for elders, for teachers and for people in the community. That's why we think it's very important that our children should come to evening schools.

There's a partnership with parents in bringing up their children, of course. We Muslims believe – and I'm sure people of other faiths believe the same – that education starts at home. We start teaching our kids from a very young age about their faith and how they should behave as Muslims: what to say, what not to say, how to eat, how to sit.

FACT-FINDER

Qur'an
Islam's sacred book revealed by Allah to the Prophet Muhammad (Peace be upon him).

Urdu
Main language spoken in Pakistan.

11

NAME: *Andleeb S*

WHAT I DO: *I'm fourteen years old and go to a Catholic school. Me, Mum and Dad, all three of us chose the school. Mum chose it because there are no schools nearby that are mixed or boys' schools. Some people think that if there's a boys' school nearby it could be distracting for girls.*

SOME OF MY SPECIAL INTERESTS: *I like playing hockey. That's my favourite sport. My favourite subjects are Biology, Chemistry and Latin.*

MORE ABOUT ME

I go to mosque in the evening on weekdays. Some of the others there sometimes ask, 'Which school do you go to?' When I tell them, they say, 'Aren't you lonely without other Muslim girls there?' No, I'm not. You have to mix with other people, not just people of your own religion. You need an outward view of life which takes in other people's attitudes.

My best friend's Sandeep. She's Sikh, and we hang around a lot together. My friend Melissa's Hindu. Suki and Madeleine, two other girls in my class, weren't baptized when they were born. They don't have a religion. Maddy's really open about religion. She doesn't oppose other religions. She really speaks her mind, and I respect her for that.

In Islam, there's a requirement for a woman's body to be covered. What happened about school uniform was that Mum asked the Headmistress if I could wear trousers – we call them pyjamah – under my skirt. Mum also asked if I could wear a long skirt on top. The Headmistress was really nice about it. She said I could provided the pyjamah was the same colour as the tights the other girls wore. So in summer they wear white tights and I wear white pyjamah. In the winter, when they wear cream tights, I wear cream pyjamah. The first time I went to school dressed like this, the others said, 'Look what Andleeb's wearing.' So I told them it was part of my religion to do it. They accept I'm a Muslim. They think it's quite normal.

When I play hockey, sometimes I wear tracksuit bottoms and sometimes I wear a skirt. But that's different. It's a girls' school. The teacher's a woman. There are no boys or men around, so there's no obligation for me to be covered in the same way.

My mum doesn't like listening to pop music. She doesn't like music about love and stuff like that. We shouldn't be listening to things like that in a Muslim house. It's a way for the Devil to lead you into doing wrong. Muslims should pray to Allah five times a day. Listening to songs and things like that distract you from worshipping Allah. They distract you from doing the good things which in Allah's eyes are rewardable, which we'll be rewarded for at the Day of Judgement.

I want to go into medicine and become a doctor: a hospital doctor, a general surgeon in fact. Helping other people is so important. People are dying because others don't notice they need help or aren't willing to help. They get taken off hospital waiting lists because someone thinks they're too old to bother about. It doesn't matter who you are or how old you are, your needs matter as much as anyone else's. Everyone should be treated the same.

FACT-FINDER

Catholic school
School run by Roman Catholic Christians.

Baptized when born
For Roman Catholics, being baptized is the first stage in becoming a member of the church. Most Catholic parents have their children baptized when they are babies.

Day of Judgement
When everyone, not just Muslims, will be judged by Allah. (See also page 43.)

NAME: *Musarat S*

MY FAMILY: *I'm the mother of two children, aged fourteen and sixteen.*

MY ROLE IN THE RELIGIOUS COMMUNITY: *I teach in the Sparkbrook Islamic Centre – evening classes. That's every weekday. I teach Islamic and Qur'anic Studies to girls of all ages. This Sunday, we're giving out trophies to the children for achievement in their studies.*

I also teach Urdu because Urdu is my mother tongue. I can speak Punjabi as well, Pakistani Punjabi and Indian Punjabi.

SOME OF MY SPECIAL INTERESTS

Out of my interests, I enjoy sewing, but I also like cooking. I can sew almost anything – things for the house, like cushions – and I do embroidery. I embroider my daughter Andleeb's dresses and sometimes put beads on them. She wore one recently on a trip to London – it was light bluish with red beads. Her friends couldn't believe that I'd made it myself.

I also sew everyday things, like shalwar-kameez. That's what we women usually wear. Sometimes I'll sew a long dress for Andleeb when she wants to wear different clothes. In Islam, a woman is not allowed to uncover any part of her body or wear tight-fitting clothes. She should be covered from her head to her ankles, with only her hands, face and feet revealed. So Andleeb can wear a long skirt and a jumper or a long dress if she likes.

Men, on the other hand, must wear clothing which covers them from navel to knees, even in hot countries. They need to wear more than that in Britain!

FACT-FINDER

Qur'anic
The Qur'an is Islam's sacred book revealed by Allah to the Prophet Muhammad (Peace be upon him).

Mother tongue • Urdu
Urdu is the main language of Pakistan. Musarat means that her family spoke Urdu before they came to Britain. They still use Urdu at home as well as English.

Punjabi
Language spoken by people from the Punjab, a region in north-west India and south-east Pakistan.

Shalwar-kameez
A long-sleeved tunic (kameez) reaching nearly to the knee worn over loose trousers (shalwar) gathered into a close-fitting band at the ankle.

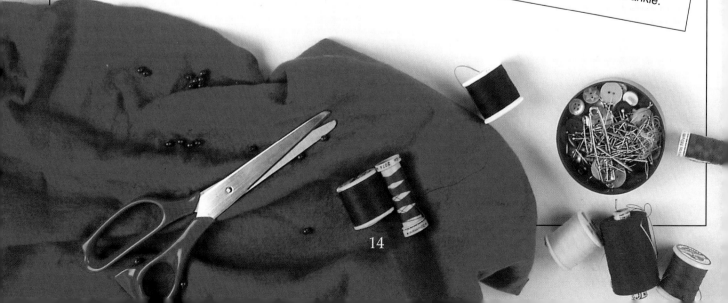

WHERE I BELONG

I was born in Pakistan and I belong to Pakistan. But before I am Pakistani, I am Muslim. Being a Muslim is more important to me. I was born into a Muslim family and I hope I am living my life as a practising Muslim.

I don't think it matters where you live. You can practise your faith wherever you are. I think that would be true of any person of faith. Of course, your practice may differ if you live in a place where the majority of people are not of your faith. You have to be more careful then. You have to struggle more. In Britain, Muslims have to be careful when we buy anything edible. There are certain things which we are not allowed to eat or drink. Even buying sweets, for instance, we need to look carefully at the ingredients to make sure they don't contain animal fat. In a Muslim country, you don't have to bother about that. Everyone is following the same requirements, so you can take things like food being allowable a lot more for granted.

I found the first few years I was in Britain very hard in this respect. Now there's an established Muslim community, things are much better. As a Muslim, you can get most of the things you need quite easily now.

MUHAMMAD AFZAL

FACT-FINDER

Don't contain animal fat
Muslims may eat meat and other animal products but they must follow the Qur'an's instructions about what animals and what methods of slaughter are halal (permitted). In a non-Muslim country, they cannot assume that the ingredients of a foodstuff like 'animal fat' will be halal.

I feel in my heart that I'm Pakistani and I want to be in Pakistan. I wish some-how that I could live there, but we can't afford it. It's easier for Ibrar. He's got his parents here, his brothers, their children, his friends. He's lived here all his life. He grew up in this country. He speaks the language. In fact, his English is better than his Urdu.

FACT-FINDER

Urdu
Main language spoken in Pakistan.

I've got no relations here apart from a niece, no close relatives. My parents are still in Pakistan. We do go and see them, though, from time to time.

FARZANA K

Where do I belong? I'm not very sure about that. I love the country where I was born and where I spent my childhood – that's Pakistan. I was twelve when I first came to Britain. I didn't like it at first. I arrived at the beginning of January, when it was dark and rainy and snowy, very different to Pakistan. In Pakistan, the days are mostly long and sunny. It rains in certain months, in August and September, but that's the only rainy season. At other times there's very little rain. Even in winter it's dry and warm and sunny. People sit outside in the sun to do their household chores. My mum had a portable cooker which she used to take outside when it was sunny. Everybody would sit outside in the sun to eat.

When I first came to Britain, I found it very boring by compari-son. Now, having spent most of my life here, I enjoy it. But actually I don't have very much choice. The children were born here and they love this country. When we go to Pakistan for holidays, which we do occasionally, we do enjoy being there for a short while. I'm not sure what we'd feel about being there long term.

So I have a great love for Pakistan, but I have special attachments to this country, too.

MUSARAT S

I feel torn, actually, about this. I came to Britain when I was seven. The first generation of people to come from Pakistan – that's my father's generation – had a dream that one day they'd go back. My father told me it was his intention to come here for two years. He wanted to earn enough money to be able to go back to Pakistan and buy two oxen and ploughing gear, so that he could live on the land of his fathers. But he came here and he got trapped.

This same dream was instilled by people like my parents into my generation: we should try to earn enough money to go back to Pakistan and live happily ever after. But it doesn't work that way. I've been back to Pakistan a few times to try it out and it's very difficult. The feeling I get is that people in Pakistan see us as foreigners. In their language, we're *walethi*, British. It's not an uncomplimentary word, not like being called 'Paki' in Britain. But it shows that people in Pakistan don't see us staying there permanently. They know that we won't be there for long. When the money runs out, we'll escape to Britain again.

I've said this to my father, and he doesn't like it: 'To tell you the truth, Dad, we're never going to go back. It's only a dream. It's your dream and you've brainwashed it into me and my generation.' But that dream's still there. Part of me believes I could go back, another part knows it's impossible. For instance, my children have grown up used to a certain standard of living which they wouldn't get in Pakistan. But there's still this voice inside me and every so often it says, 'How about going back?'

I did go back to Pakistan recently. I took special leave and went for ten months with the whole family. There were bad floods in Pakistan in 1993, and we decided to go out and do voluntary relief work in the villages. We saved about £10 000 for this. After ten months in Pakistan it had all been spent. On any given day, someone in my family would be ill – one of the children or me or my wife. Also, I just didn't have the means to do relief work on my own. You need to be backed by a big organization like Muslim Aid or Islamic Relief. When you've helped one person, another will say, 'I want help next.' Soon there's a queue, and if you haven't got the resources to cope, all you can do is run away. In the end I had just enough money to buy tickets to bring us home.

IBRAR K

I reckon I belong in the Islamic community, but not only in the Islamic community. Islam for me is the best religion, but I want to get a bigger picture of life as well. I don't just want Islamic views on everything. I want to get an understanding of all religions. I want to see what they believe in and what they think is right.

In the U.K., there's freedom of expression, and that includes religious expression. Some countries have strict censorship. You've got to respect this country for the freedom it gives people.

My parents come from Pakistan, so I feel I have ties there. I have some contact with my relatives in Pakistan by telephone, and we write to each other. I've been to Pakistan three times now. After I've done my A-levels, I intend to go back. I'll be just in time for the cricket World Cup!

I do feel, though, that I belong in Britain. I was born here. This is the society I belong to. I've studied here. In fact, one of the things I've studied is English Law. My friends are here. My ambitions are here.

But I do have a Muslim identity, first and foremost. So number one, I'm a British Muslim, then secondly I'm a Pakistani living in Britain.

IFZAL A

WHAT I FEEL STRONGLY ABOUT

I feel very strongly about my family. I want to see my children educated and successful and happy. If they are happy, I am happy. Parents have a big responsibility. If a mother and father can't look after their children and see that they get what they need, who else will?

I like to see Muslim children growing up with a strong understanding of their religion. When this doesn't happen, when you see Muslim children drifting away from their religion, I'd say this was their parents' fault. I don't think you can blame the children. The parents have most influence, or they should have. It's their job to bring up their children to be good people and good Muslims. That's regardless of the society they may be living in. Parents can't blame their children and they can't blame society if they fail in this duty.

I sent all my children to evening school at Sparkbrook Islamic Centre from when they were small. My husband worked away from Birmingham, so I took them there myself. I think that's laid the foundations for them. That's why they know so much about their religion and their culture now. I think I've done a good job for them.

NAZIR A

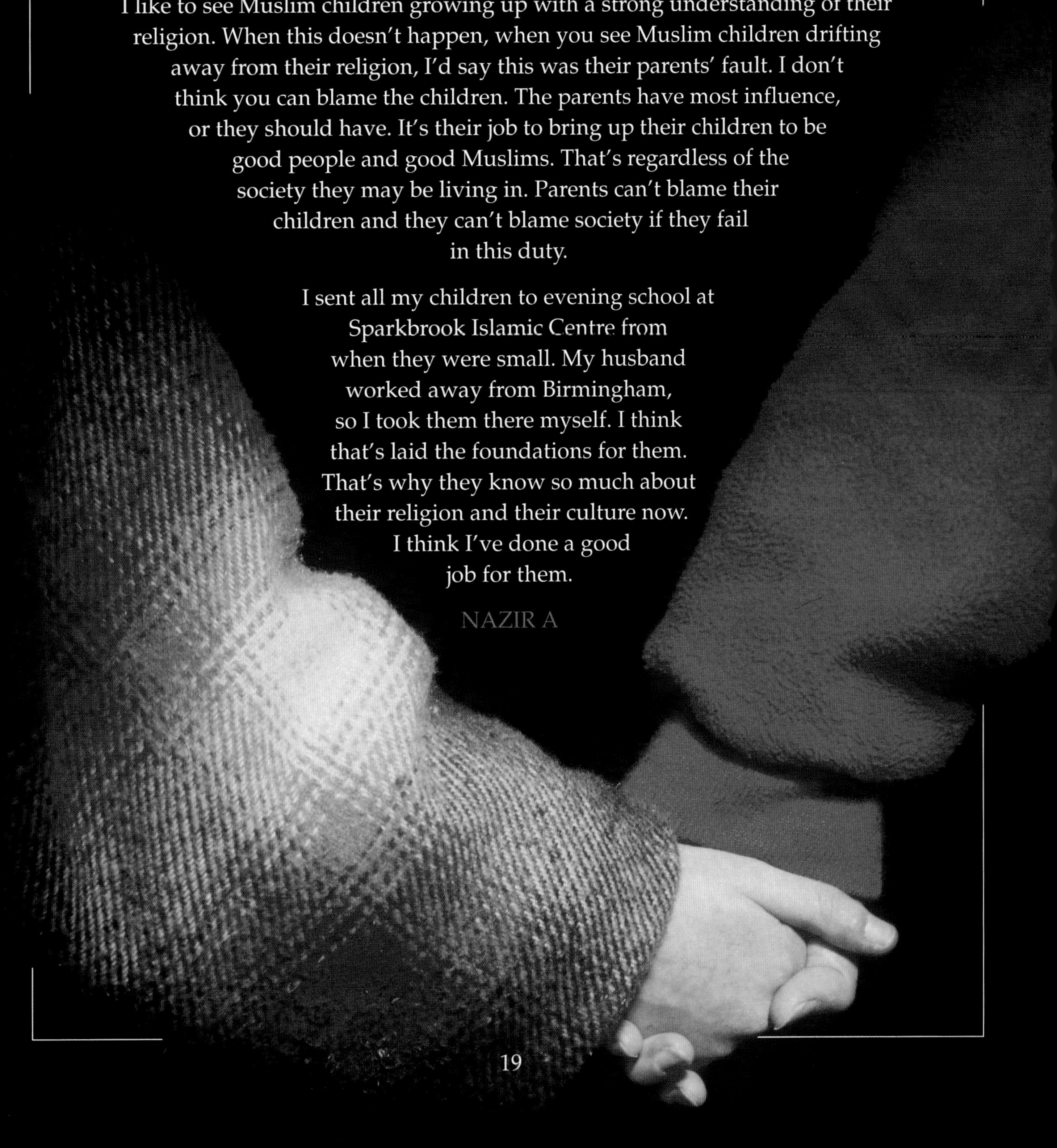

19

I feel strongly about Asian people, especially Pakistani people, not educating their daughters. Often they get their daughters married at an early age, like at sixteen or seventeen. Even if the girls are good students, they get taken out of education.

I went into a secondary school the other day and the Deputy Head said that the school was deeply concerned about this. The girls can be really interested in what they're doing at school, motivated to get a good education, but their parents won't allow them to. This leaves a Muslim girl with no choice – she obeys her parents. Quite a lot of parents don't really trust their daughters because of the atmosphere the girls find around them as they grow up. Parents worry that their daughters will meet and marry someone without their approval, without an arranged marriage. There's a lot of stigma attached to that. Their worst fear is that their Muslim daughter will marry a non-Muslim.

This attitude of parents used to be a problem in Pakistan, too, but not nowadays. In Pakistan, parents are more conscious than they are here that their children, even their daughters, need a good education. When I was growing up, a lot of people thought that educating daughters was just foolish. The daughters would be getting married and doing household work, so why educate them?

I think that's wrong, and it's proved to be wrong. In a lot of families in Britain today, both parents have to work to keep a decent standard of living. Where the father only is able to work, I think there's often a lot of hardship.

When I was seventeen, my parents arranged a marriage for me. I was in college, and my education stopped. I've always felt that deficiency. I look at my brothers and sisters: one sister became a doctor in Pakistan, another sister is a graduate teaching at a college, my youngest sister recently did an MSc in Physics, my brother qualified as a doctor two years ago, my younger brother is an engineer in Pakistan. I do feel strongly that I missed out.

MUSARAT S

I feel strongly about women's rights. Nowadays, women seem to be treated like things, like animals. A woman doesn't listen to her husband so he pours petrol over her and sets her alight. The case goes to court and he just gets a fine. You see these stories in the news, and I think it's just so unfair.

Islam has given Muslim women a lot of rights. The Prophet Muhammad (Peace be upon him) said to the unbelievers in Arafat when he was about to die: 'Be kind to your wives, because they are your partners now and for ever.' I think there's a big difference between being a partner and being treated as a slave to work around the house.

I want to grow up to be someone who puts a Muslim woman's view over to other people. I want them to understand that Muslim girls have a life that should be respected. For example, one of my friends is getting married today. She's sixteen. Her sister's getting married today. She's eighteen. Their mother was thirteen when she was married in Pakistan. This is an issue about Asian culture. Some Asian Muslim parents think that if you have a daughter, the best thing is to get her married off quickly. They don't marry their sons off in the same way. Once the girl's married, she goes to live in her in-laws' home. It's as if she's been got rid of by her own family.

That friend of mine is now going to be pretty helpless. She won't be able to do much. She won't be able to go out. Her education's been stopped early so she'll find it hard if she has to get a job to earn money for her kids. She could be in a right mess if her husband loses his job. Her life could end up being absolute misery.

ANDLEEB'S

FACT-FINDER

Arafat
Plain near Makkah. One of the sites visited by Muslim pilgrims during the Hajj.

I feel strongly about my rights. I think everyone should have equal opportunities. There should be no bias on grounds of religion or race or culture. Personally, I think there's a lot of religious bias in Britain: less racial bias now, more religious bias. It's at the workplace, in places of power. There seems to be a lot of anti-Islamic propaganda at the moment, and an anti-Islamic media.

What's happening is that people are picking up some of the words they hear or read in the media and they're using them without thinking what they mean. For example, at work I was described as a 'fundamentalist', a 'fanatical fundamentalist'. This was in a report. I couldn't believe it! The person who wrote this about me said he didn't believe in God. I think that was part of the problem. I was a practising Muslim, and he couldn't accept that. He didn't understand it.

I said to him: 'What do you mean by "fundamentalist"? Is a fundamentalist someone with a gun in their hand telling others to become Muslim? Or is it someone who devoutly follows their belief, whatever that belief may be? If it's the second then, yes, you're right, I am a fundamentalist. But the two things aren't the same.' He didn't have an answer.

As Muslims, we believe that prayer five times a day is obligatory. When we reach adulthood, we have to do it, wherever we are. For believers, missing prayers is a major sin.

FACT-FINDER

Sin
Here, action that breaks Allah's laws.

Qur'an
Islam's sacred book revealed by Allah to the Prophet Muhammad (Peace be upon him).

Ten Commandments
The ten rules given by God to Moses, known as Prophet Musa in Islam. Muslims do not have to obey all of the Ten Commandments listed in the Bible (see Exodus 20:1–17).

I never miss my prayers, even at work. But I don't cause any difficulties for my employers either. I pray in my own time, during dinner and tea breaks. I'm not in anybody's way. Whenever they need me, I'm there. But I get the feeling that my colleagues don't like it. They'd prefer to be working with someone who swears when they swear, who puts pin-ups on the wall. I'm not like that so I'm a bit of an outsider to them. This is ironical really, because in Victorian times in this country, if you weren't religious and didn't go to church, people thought you were odd. Now it's totally the opposite.

During my first eight years doing the job I do, I worked with other religious people – mostly Christians. We got on quite well because we all had something we believed in. Now I work with people who don't believe in anything, really. The hardest part is trying to be a practising Muslim in that type of environment. It's like being in the same room as people who are smoking when you don't smoke and you don't want to breathe in other people's smoke. For instance, when there are no women around there's a lot of talk about sex, and such degrading things are said. I said to one colleague who was looking at pictures in a men's magazine: 'That could be your daughter. It could be your wife or your sister. Would you still be looking at them then?' He said, 'It's their life. They can do whatever they like.' I think it's an influence from Satan, from the Devil, that makes my colleagues behave like that. He's whispering in their ears and he's running in their blood. He's telling them to do these evil things, to talk evil, speak evil and hear evil.

What keeps me going is my faith. I know that on the Day of Judgement I will have to answer to God for everything I do. My colleagues will, too. Sometimes I tell them: 'You can do whatever you like in this world, but one day you will have to answer to a judge who does not take bribes. You will not be able to avoid him until you answer all his questions. Everything you have – life, possessions, family – he has given you. You will have to show him how you've used these things.'

Once someone said, 'Suppose on the Day of Judgement we're all forgiven and sent to Paradise, then you've lost out.' Muslims do believe that the mercy of God outstrips his anger, but it won't work like that. What God will do on the Day of Judgement, as it says in the Qur'an, is to forgive our minor sins if we have avoided the major ones. Some of the major sins are listed in the Ten Commandments, and not believing your God is one God is *the* major sin in Islam. But there will be a Day of Judgement.

I find all this a challenge, but actually I like it sometimes. I never start a discussion at work about religion. In fact, we've jokingly made a pact. I won't talk about religion as long as they don't talk about sex. But they don't keep their side of the promise. They do try, but then they see a woman walking by and the remarks start up again.

IBRAR K

One of the impressions that seems to be being given by the media is that Islam is a hard religion, a harsh religion. It comes out too in some of the questions that visitors ask when they come to the Centre. Often there's talk of fundamentalism and things like that.

When I look at Islam, what I see is a religion that is for peace and harmony. One of the meanings of the word 'Islam' is 'peace, submission and obedience'. By accepting Islam, we as Muslims are submitting to the will of Allah, we're doing what God wants us to. God doesn't ask for anything that is harsh, which we can't do or we can't achieve. So we believe that if we follow Islam and practise Islam, then we will live in peace in this life and in the life hereafter. Love and peace are two very basic teachings of Islam.

Sparkbrook is an area of very high unemployment, but we've never had any conflict here. Muslims and Christians have always lived together in peace and harmony. I don't think this is just a happy accident. Centres like ours and counterparts in other faith communities locally work together on community issues like unemployment and health. I don't think any of us are blinkered or inward looking. We meet each other, try to understand each other. I would say Sparkbrook is a good example of positive relations between Muslims and Christians.

We're sitting in an Islamic Centre. There's a mosque at the back. There's also a pub down the road! I can't remember us ever having had any problems.

MUHAMMAD AFZAL

FACT-FINDER

Fundamentalism
Term often used in an uncomplimentary way to describe the views and actions of religious groups regarded as strict, extreme or even fanatical. (See also page 22.)

I feel strongly about my fellow Muslims, basically. Not just Muslims in Britain but Muslims all over the world, like in Bosnia. The charity Islamic Relief is organizing shelter, clothing and some of the basic necessities for the Bosnian Muslims. I'm involved with that quite actively. I feel that, as fellow Muslims, we have a duty there which we can't just let go. We can't just sit and watch our fellow Muslims suffering like that and do nothing.

FACT-FINDER

Ummah
Literally 'community'. Term used to describe the whole community of Muslims worldwide.

The Prophet Muhammad (Peace be upon him) said that, wherever they are in the world, Muslims are one ummah, one body. It's like a human body. If one part of the body hurts, the whole body feels the pain. My personal view is that Muslims are slowly drifting away from this idea. Muslim politicians aren't doing much about Bosnia. Muslim countries like Saudi Arabia seem to be keeping their heads down. I just can't understand their attitude. When you see all the Muslim brothers and sisters suffering there in Bosnia, I think it's unbelievable. I think it's down to laziness, that attitude. The Muslim identity is drifting away.

IFZAL A

MY FAVOURITE FESTIVAL

I d-ul-Fitr and Id-ul-Adha are both important: Id-ul-Fitr because it's the end of Ramadan and Id-ul-Adha because of Hajj and the sacrifices people make.

In this country, you don't see sacrifices at Id-ul-Adha, but in Pakistan you actually see them out in the open. You see people taking their goat (or a cow or an ox or whatever) down to open ground to sacrifice it. When the animal has been sacrificed, you prepare the meat and divide it into three parts. One is for the immediate family, one is for the wider family and one is to be distributed to poor people in the area. So the meat is shared out, and there's a lot of excitement as you're doing it.

Sacrificing is different here. You give your order to the local Muslim meat shop a few days ahead of Id-ul-Adha and it gets passed on to the halal meat factory. They then slaughter an animal on your behalf either on Id-ul-Adha itself or up to two days later, because there are three days of sacrificing altogether. If the sacrifice doesn't happen on one of those three days, it's not the sacrifice of Ibrahim. But you don't see the sacrifice in this country. All you get is the chopped-up meat, ready to cook with.

Generally, I look forward to meeting relatives at festival times, getting together, buying new clothes for the children, preparing food for people. This all gives you a feeling of happiness. There's a lot of anticipation. Children are getting excited, waiting for the money to come. At our Ids, we give money to the children, so they're all holding their purses out!

FARZANA K

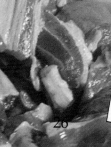

FACT-FINDER

Ramadan
The ninth Islamic month, when Muslims fast from food and drink every day from just before dawn until sunset.

Hajj
Annual pilgrimage to Makkah. All Muslims should go on Hajj at least once in their lifetime provided that their health is good enough and they have sufficient money to do so.

Halal meat factory
'Halal' means permitted by the laws of Islam. This factory will use the approved Muslim procedure for slaughtering animals for meat.

Ibrahim
Abraham, who was asked by God to sacrifice his son. (See also page 30.)

26

M y favourite festival is Id-ul-Adha, the 'Big Id'. It celebrates the time when Ibrahim (Peace be upon him) was going to sacrifice his son Ishma'il (Peace be upon him) to show his devotion to God, but a lamb was sacrificed instead.

The Big Id I really remember was when we were in Pakistan when I was seven. It was really good. It was the first time I'd been to Pakistan and my grandfather sacrificed a cow. He sent me inside because he didn't want me to see everything, though.

The sacrifice is important. It shows God that we're faithful to him, like Ibrahim (Peace be upon him), and that we haven't forgotten him. Poor people are remembered, too. A third of the meat is distributed to poor people in the area.

When you sacrifice a small animal, like a lamb, it's just one person's sacrifice. A cow is a sacrifice for seven people. That means that seven people share the blessing. You have sort of shares. The cow that my grandfather sacrificed was also on behalf of my grandmother and my mother and other people in the family.

Muslims believe what is written in the Qur'an. It tells us that Allah has said human beings are his most important creation, and that everything else is created for human beings. We are allowed to sacrifice animals so that we can eat. We don't feel guilty about eating the things that Allah has permitted us to eat.

ANDLEEB S

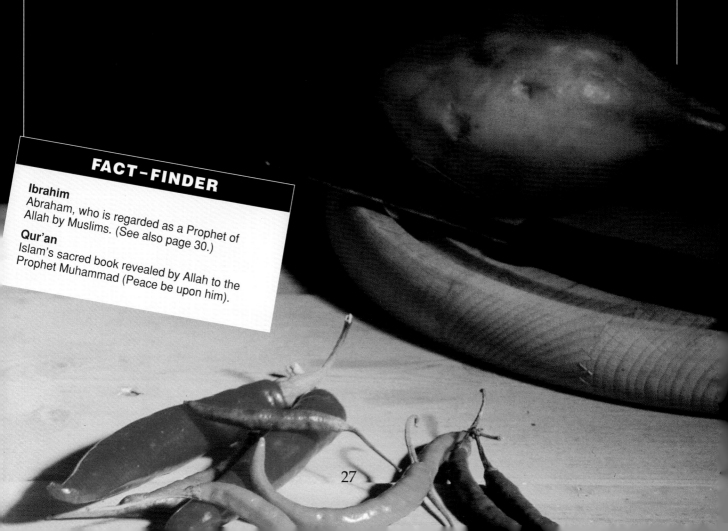

FACT-FINDER

Ibrahim
Abraham, who is regarded as a Prophet of Allah by Muslims. (See also page 30.)

Qur'an
Islam's sacred book revealed by Allah to the Prophet Muhammad (Peace be upon him).

There are two main festivals in the Muslim faith, and to me they're both important, for different reasons. The first is the festival of fast-breaking, Id-ul-Fitr. Before the festival, Muslims fast from dawn to sunset every day for twenty-nine or thirty days. Fasting means refraining from eating, drinking, even smoking.

Apart from being one of our basic duties, one of the Five Pillars of Islam, fasting makes us realize what it feels like to be hungry and poor. It gives a feeling of what it must be like for millions of people all over the world who go without food every day. It makes us realize how lucky we are that we have enough food to be able to choose what we're going to eat. It's something we especially remind the children about. When you give them food, children have a habit of saying, 'Oh, Mum, I don't like that!' At this time particularly, we remind the children of what they've seen on television – famine in Ethiopia or Bangladesh, perhaps. We remind them that they should be thankful to God for the gifts he has given them.

At the end of this month of fasting, on the day of Id-ul-Fitr, there's a kind of satisfaction and gratitude towards God that we have fulfilled one of our basic duties. It is one of the happiest times for a Muslim. Muslims are told that whenever we do good in this world, there is a reward for it from God, but the reward for fasting is unlimited. God has said that he will give the reward himself to those people who fast. If I have to compare the two Ids, I would say that Id-ul-Fitr is possibly more significant than the festival of sacrifice, Id-ul-Adha.

Id-ul-Fitr is a day of gifts and giving. In the morning, before we do anything else, we go to Id prayers. We eat something before we go, usually something sweet, because that is the tradition of the Prophet. We wear our best clothes. After the Id prayers are finished, people in the congregation meet each other and embrace each other, then they come home. The children are given gifts and money and we send food to our neighbours, whether they are Muslim or not – it doesn't matter. People also go out and meet their friends and relatives.

MUHAMMAD AFZAL

FACT-FINDER

Id-ul-Adha
See also page 27.

Prophet
Here, Muhammad, the final Prophet of Islam.

T here are two Ids in Islam, and I like them both. The thing about having just two Ids is they can both be special, like Christmas and Easter for Christians. You wait for the festivals and you look forward to them. They're like a reward. So the Ids are joyous occasions.

What do I do at Id? I cook! Food is important on these days. It's part of celebrating Id to offer food and hospitality. We visit each other – friends and relatives. We wear new clothes. We exchange gifts.

Both Ids come after we've performed special duties for Allah's sake. One comes after fasting during Ramadan and the other after Hajj. I haven't been on pilgrimage, but I do pray to God that I will have the chance. When God wants me to go, I will go.

NAZIR A

FACT-FINDER

Id
Term meaning 'recurring happiness' used for the two main Muslim festivals.

Ramadan
The ninth Islamic month, when Muslims fast from food and drink every day from just before dawn until sunset.

Hajj
Annual pilgrimage to Makkah. All Muslims should go on Hajj at least once in their lifetime provided that their health is good enough and they have sufficient money to do so.

My favourite festival would have to be Id-ul-Adha, known as the 'Big Id', which occurs after the pilgrimage. I don't know whether you've ever seen the pilgrimage taking place. I think it's amazing. We watch it on satellite TV – we tune in to Saudi Arabian television so we can see it. It's an amazing sight. People of different races and nationalities, from different backgrounds, all dressed in special white robes – ihram, they're called – all completely equal. It doesn't matter if you're a king or a peasant, on Hajj everyone is equal. It gives me a buzz, just to see that – Ummah, one united body of Muslims. When I see it, I say, 'Yes, that's want I want to do.' One day I will go. That's definite.

Id-ul-Adha is celebrated at home and at the mosque. Obviously, we go to Id prayers first thing in the morning, normally at about half-past seven. For Id prayers I like to go to Birmingham Central Mosque. I mean, I go to Sparkbrook Islamic Centre to study, and I do pray there mostly, but for Id prayers I want to be part of a larger gathering of people. You can fit over two thousand people into the Central Mosque. Once again, it gives me a buzz to read and pray with a congregation that size.

At Id-ul-Adha people sacrifice a lamb if they can afford to. The sacrificing originates from the days of Ibrahim (Peace be upon him). God wanted to test Ibrahim's faith and asked him to sacrifice his son. So Ibrahim (Peace be upon him) went out with Ishma'il. As Ibrahim's sword was coming down towards Ishma'il, the Angel Jibril in a split second replaced Ishma'il with a ram. It was the ram that Ibrahim's blade struck. This was a test of Ibrahim's faith. The story appears in the Bible but it's also written in the Qur'an. It is a reminder to Muslims that we should be prepared to sacrifice everything that is most precious to us for Allah.

IFZAL A

FACT-FINDER

Pilgrimage • Hajj
The annual pilgrimage to Makkah. All Muslims should go on Hajj at least once in their lifetime provided that their health is good enough and they have sufficient money to do so.

Ummah
Literally 'community'. Term used to describe the whole community of Muslims worldwide.

Ibrahim • Jibril • Bible • Qur'an
This story about Ibrahim (Abraham) appears in Surah 37:81–113 of the Qur'an, Islam's sacred book. In the Bible version (see Genesis 22:1–19), Abraham nearly sacrifices Isaac, his younger son, and the angel's name is Gabriel.

Two festivals are significant. There's Id-ul-Fitr, which celebrates the end of the month of Ramadan, and there's Id-ul-Adha, the festival that ends Hajj. Hajj continues what we call the tradition of Ibrahim. Even if you don't go on Hajj, you celebrate the tradition of Ibrahim at Id-ul-Adha. Id-ul-Adha is the 'Big Id'. It follows about two-and-a-half months after the 'Small Id', Id-ul-Fitr.

On Id-ul-Fitr, we get up early. Everyone has a bath and puts on new clothes. I go to the mosque with the boys to say morning prayers behind an imam. We go to the mosque at Sparkbrook Islamic Centre. That's where all my family go – my father, my brothers. After morning prayers, everybody greets each other. Some people – close relatives, usually – hug each other, others will shake hands.

The younger generation also asks the older generation for forgiveness for anything they may have done to hurt them during the year. We believe that if our fathers are happy with us, God is happy with us. We also believe that Paradise lies under our mothers' feet. So parents are to be respected, and Id-ul-Fitr is one of the times when you can ask your parents to forgive you.

You can ask other people for forgiveness, too. People are always sinning. We back-bite. Sometimes we're dishonest. So on this day, you find the people who you think you might have wronged during the previous year and ask them for forgiveness. They're usually happy on Id-ul-Fitr, so they'll say, 'I forgive you.' Even if they don't, if in their hearts they're happy, that is forgiveness. So Id-ul-Fitr is a time to make friends with everybody, settle differences. It's a very good time.

IBRAR K

FACT–FINDER

Ramadan
The ninth Islamic month, when Muslims fast from food and drink every day from just before dawn until sunset.

Hajj
Annual pilgrimage to Makkah. All Muslims should go on Hajj at least once in their lifetime provided that their health is good enough and they have sufficient money to do so.

Ibrahim
Abraham, who is regarded as a Prophet of Allah by Muslims. (See also opposite.)

Imam
Literally 'leader'. Here, person who leads communal prayer at the mosque.

Paradise
Heaven, where Muslims hope Allah will send them on the Day of Judgement as a reward for living a good life. (See also page 23.)

Sinning
Doing wrong, breaking Allah's laws.

A SPECIAL MOMENT

My wedding was a special moment. Before it I was anxious. I didn't know what Ibrar would be like, what his family would be like. I'd met Ibrar's mother and father before, but you don't know people properly until you mix with them. I hadn't seen Ibrar before the wedding, not even a photograph. He saw me but I didn't see him.

It all happened very quickly. Ibrar didn't want to marry the person that his parents wanted him to marry, so they arranged somebody else, and that was me. They showed him my picture and he agreed. But because I come from a very orthodox family, I didn't want to see his photograph. I couldn't have seen his photo.

Our way of arranged marriage means that we have to build a new life together. We have to work at that. You build the marriage then grow inside it to meet the other person. It's different to a love match, where you start out knowing the other person then see if it's possible to turn that relationship into a marriage.

Usually, in Pakistan, a wedding lasts for three days. That's partly because there are a lot of traditions associated with it which have come from Hindu culture. The official part, preparing the nikkah, the marriage certificate, is done a few days earlier. Ibrar and I sat in two different rooms. The imam asked me three times if I accepted Ibrar, and I said yes. The imam asked Ibrar if he accepted me, and he said yes. The traditional celebrations came later.

On the first day, I had my hair made up. Oil was put into it and my hands and feet were decorated. The second day, our parents gave a big dinner. There were several hundred guests. That's a usual number. In the old days, when Ibrar's father was married, for example, an entire village could be invited to a wedding dinner. The caller would announce

the wedding from the top of the minaret and say that everyone was invited to the party. Two or three buffaloes would be sacrificed. There'd be rice and chappatis and other food. Everyone would eat, then say a blessing for the wedding.

After the wedding dinner, I was taken from my old home to my new home. Brides used to be carried in a dhori, which is a sort of chair with poles, but I went in a car. There was quite a procession – cars, buses.

I wore red for my wedding. That's a Hindu custom really. There's no Muslim religious requirement that a woman should get married in red. Ibrar wore a creamy shirt and white trousers.

Hajj was also a special moment. I went with Ibrar. I was so happy there that I wished we had enough money to go every year. It is a place that is so special. The pilgrimage site is a very blessed place and you know that it's blessed. You can feel it. After the Hajj was over, we went to see the Tomb of the Prophet (Peace be upon him) in Madinah. There, I had another strong feeling, this time of being close to a father figure – the father of a nation.

FARZANA K

T he most memorable moment in my life was when I went to Pakistan for the first time. There are big gates to the family house in Pakistan. We went through the gates and all the family on my mum's side came running out to meet us. I'd seen my nan before, but none of the others. I was meeting them for the first time and I was just so pleased, I really was. I was seven then.

We were on holiday, but we extended our visit because we wanted to stay longer. It was really good fun. I was very upset when we left.

I'm not sure whether I'd like to live there. It's very hot. But I do like it. I feel I've got roots there.

ANDLEEB S

FACT-FINDER

Imam
Literally 'leader'. Here, person who leads communal prayer at the mosque and performs other Muslim religious ceremonies.

Caller • Minaret
A minaret is a tall tower attached to a mosque from which the mu'adhin (caller) calls Muslims to prayer five times a day.

Prophet
Here, Muhammad, the final Prophet of Islam.

This special moment happened just two weeks ago. Every Friday evening I go to the Central Mosque in Birmingham. There's a study circle there for learning about the teaching of the Prophet. We also learn some Hadith, sayings of the Prophet. Then after that we have a da'wah session. Some of the Muslim brothers, we go out and preach Islam. Usually we talk to Muslims who have gone astray, who aren't following the straight path. So we go to the places where they gather.

This particular evening, one of the brothers came up with the idea of going to one of the Asian snooker-halls. So we went to a snooker-hall not far from here. It was packed. There were some Hindus and Sikhs but mainly Muslims. One of the brothers, Rashid, has a fairly good knowledge of Islam. He's studying Law at Birmingham University, so he's pretty good at expressing himself. We went in and put Rashid up on a crate. He looked about seven feet tall.

Rashid started talking to the men in the hall. He spoke about Islam and about what would happen to them when they died, because death is definite – it's guaranteed for everyone. Once he started talking about death and people having to answer for their actions, the snooker stopped. Everyone froze. Their attention was focused on this one guy. About thirty men – they were Muslims – left their snooker and came over to listen to him. Somehow, by the grace of Allah, he'd had an effect on them.

After this da'wah session, Rashid asked, 'Which of you brothers would like to come back to the mosque now? Even if you don't pray five times a day, for Allah's sake pray with us today and we'll teach you some of the basics of Islam.' I couldn't believe it – they all came with us. We'd gone down there, the four of us, in two cars. On the way back there was a convoy of at least ten behind us!

We took the men to Sparkbrook Islamic Centre. We read the isha prayers – that was at about eleven o'clock. They stayed with us until half-past two in the morning, asking us questions about Islam. We told them what we were able to, about the basic qualities of Islam.

The whole thing was amazing. There must have been some good in those men's hearts. It was an experience that really moved me.

IFZAL A

FACT-FINDER

Prophet
Here, Muhammad (Peace be upon him), the final Prophet of Islam.

Da'wah
Calling people to follow Islam by preaching (as here) or by demonstrating Islam through one's actions.

Muslim brothers
Fellow (male) Muslims, not Ifzal's actual brothers.

Grace of Allah
The mercy, kindness or favour of Allah, i.e. Allah's help.

Isha prayers
One of five sets of compulsory Muslim daily prayers/worship (salah). Isha prayers should be said in the evening, before midnight.

I think one particularly special moment was when my son passed the 11-plus exam. I really wanted him to get into a grammar-school. I used to work with him in the evenings and weekends and only let him watch certain programmes on the TV. For him, I worked in a factory for one and a half years. This was to have enough money to send him to a private school for extra coaching. I thought it would not only be his failure if he did not pass, it would be mine. It was my wish that my son should go to a grammar-school. I was so pleased on the day the results came through showing he'd passed.

I remember the first time we went to the school, when they invited us. He was only ten years and a few months old. He was so little against the sixth formers. Now he's in the sixth form himself. I wish him good luck in his A-levels. My best wishes are with him.

MUSARAT S

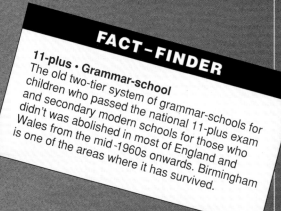

FACT-FINDER

11-plus • Grammar-school

The old two-tier system of grammar-schools for children who passed the national 11-plus exam and secondary modern schools for those who didn't was abolished in most of England and Wales from the mid-1960s onwards. Birmingham is one of the areas where it has survived.

The special moment in my life was when I went on Hajj, pilgrimage to Makkah, in 1986. I'd heard from my parents and teachers, I'd read in the Qur'an and from the Prophet's life about the Grand Mosque in Makkah, the First House of God and the Prophet's Mosque in Madinah. But when I got there and saw just in front of me the First House of Allah, the Ka'bah, I knew that this was the moment of my life. It is the wish of every Muslim to go to Makkah and see the things that they would have read and heard about. When it happened to me, it was the moment of my life.

Hajj is one of the basic duties of a Muslim, one of the Five Pillars of Islam. It's one of the most inspiring and also one of the most difficult and demanding. One of the conditions is that whoever goes on Hajj must be physically fit. Also, you should go on Hajj with your own money, and it is expensive. You can't borrow the money that takes you on Hajj.

The first thing you notice is the climate. It's very, very, very hot. Those of us who live in Britain could never imagine the heat. After every ten or fifteen minutes you need a drink of water or you wouldn't survive. Then there's the number of people, about two million, and the ritual. You can't just wander around where you like. Pilgrims have to do certain things in certain places at certain times. We're all together, and that makes going round the Ka'bah seven times or doing the fast walk from al-Safa to al-Marwah seem even more difficult. Some people are literally crushed to death.

Perhaps the most demanding and most difficult thing is throwing stones and pebbles at the three stone pillars in Mina. This year thousands of pilgrims died there. What happens is the mass of people just keeps moving towards the pillars. People at the front were trampled. When I was there, once or twice I lost my footing. I really thought I might die. But when you've completed Hajj, it's a tremendous feeling.

MUHAMMAD AFZAL

FACT-FINDER

Qur'an
Islam's sacred book revealed by Allah to the Prophet Muhammad (Peace be upon him).

Prophet
Here, Muhammad, the final Prophet of Islam.

Ka'bah
Cube-shaped building in the centre of the Grand Mosque. It was the first building constructed for worship of the One True God.

Al-Safa • Al-Marwah
Two small hills joined by a hallway. Pilgrims hurry backwards and forwards along it to remember Ishma'il's mother Hajar (Hagar) searching for water in the desert. (See Genesis 21:9–21 in the Bible.)

Pillars at Mina
These stone pillars represent the Devil.

Many special things have happened in my life, but the one that stands out is something that happened when Farzana and I were returning from Hajj. Hajj is special in itself. When I first saw the House of God, it was like an electricity bolt going through me. I didn't think I'd ever go there, but I did.

Coming back from Hajj, we stopped at a shop. I went into the shop with my wife and told the children to stay in the car. The shop was across the road from where the car was parked. Through the shop window I could see my eldest son opening the car door. Quickly I ran out of the shop and shouted to him, 'Stay there!' I don't know what must have gone through his mind, but instead he just ran across the road. A car hit him – bang! He went flying through the air for about three metres, then fell and rolled. I was watching all this. I was so shocked that for several seconds I couldn't move. Then I ran to him, and he got up.

I checked him all over for injuries – legs, arms, body, hands, face, head. Nothing. I asked him whether he was all right. He said yes, he was. And we walked away from the accident.

I personally believe that that was a gift from God. My son was given a second life.

I have no special moments really, but I have no problems either. I'm content with the life that Allah has given me. I pray to God that I should encounter no difficulties. Through prayer, I get inspiration in my life.

FACT-FINDER

Hajj
Pilgrimage to Makkah. (See opposite.)

House of God
The Ka'bah. (See opposite.)

WORDS THAT MEAN
A LOT TO ME

B asically, the whole of the Qur'an is special to me. No word is more significant than another. All of it is essential. I try to study a few paragraphs of the Qur'an every day. I try. I don't always succeed. I might forget or watch TV. I'm weak, just like everybody else.

I study the Qur'an in English because I don't totally understand Arabic. My Qur'an is in English and Arabic. It has to be, because no translation can actually encompass or comprehend what is in the Arabic. It's like a poem. If you translate a poem, you lose the feeling of it. People can get its meaning, but the original feeling won't be there. The feeling of the Qur'an is in the language it was revealed in. So I try to learn bits of the Qur'an in Arabic, but it isn't easy.

IBRAR K

FACT-FINDER

Qur'an
Islam's sacred book revealed by Allah to the Prophet Muhammad (Peace be upon him). The Angel Jibril (Gabriel) gave the Prophet the words of the Qur'an in Arabic.

B ecause I'm a Muslim, I believe in the words of Allah, the words of God, and these are contained in the Qur'an. To me, they are the most powerful words in the world.

Whenever I'm in a difficulty, I remember Allah with his words and through his names. There are ninety-nine names for Allah and we remember them for different purposes. I ask Allah to forgive me for my sins and to help me when I'm having trouble with something.
I believe he's listening.
I do believe in Allah
and I will believe
until the end.

MUSARAT S

FACT-FINDER

Sins
Wrongdoing, actions that break Allah's laws.

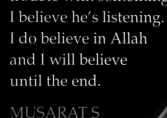

I 'm not that good at reading the Qur'an in Arabic, but I do read it regularly, and I read it all. I feel that the Qur'an is a complete thing. I don't think I could separate out any one section or verse. I don't feel that would be right. All of it is the word of God, and every word is equally important.

I study the Qur'an starting at the beginning and working through it in order. I don't dip into it for bits and pieces. I do my studying every day, from when I wake up to when the children start getting up. Every day I'll read, even if it's just a page.

Also, if one of my relatives is ill, I will read the Qur'an as a mark of respect and devotion to God, so that by his grace they may be saved from the punishment of the grave.

NAZIR A

FACT-FINDER

Qur'an
Islam's sacred book revealed by Allah to the Prophet Muhammad (Peace be upon him). The Angel Jibril (Gabriel) gave the Prophet the words of the Qur'an in Arabic.

Grace
Mercy, kindness or favour, i.e. Allah's help.

WORDS THAT MEAN A LOT TO ME

I think the word 'Allah' is the most important word to me as a Muslim. We remember Allah throughout the day because there are many points when we'll say a blessing. It is a teaching of Islam that whenever we start something – start eating, start work, get in a car to start a journey – we say, 'Bismillah-ir-Rahman-ir-Rahim.' This means: 'In the name of Allah, the Most Merciful, the Most Kind.' When we say 'Bismillah-ir-Rahman-ir-Rahim', we believe that God will help us in whatever it is we are about to do.

There are other little prayers that we say as we go about our daily lives. For instance, we say a little prayer after we've finished eating, to thank Allah, who has given us food and drink. These prayers are written down, and we teach our children at home and here at the mosque what they are: what to say when we greet somebody, when we see them off, when we go to the toilet, things like that.

MUHAMMAD AFZAL

I n the Qur'an, there's one verse which really stands out for me. It's the opening verse. In this verse, Allah tells Muslims that if there is anything we ever want, or anything we ever need, we can ask him. We just have to turn to him in prayer.

Whenever I feel distressed or there's something I really feel I need, I sit down and just ask God about it.

IFZAL A

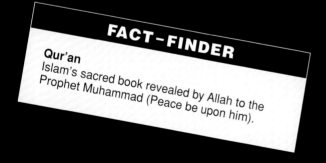

FACT-FINDER

Qur'an
Islam's sacred book revealed by Allah to the Prophet Muhammad (Peace be upon him).

I like all the words we use in our obligatory prayers and in the Qur'an. You can also pray in your own language. You say whatever you feel is necessary. You might include something you require from your Creator or something you want to happen, like good health.

There's nobody and there's nothing like Allah. I love him. I can't see him, but I know he's beneficent, merciful, master of the Day of Judgement.

We believe that there are certain things that Allah has given us freedom over and certain things that are running their course. To a Muslim, free will is not quite the same as it might be to a Christian, for example. We believe God knows everything already. He's so powerful, so infinite that he knows the past, the present and the future. He knows what we are going to do even though he has given us the free will to choose. We have been given two paths, the good and the bad. We can do what we think is right or we can do what is wrong. The choice is ours. But because of his power, God knows the choice we will make. If you believe that God does not know what you are going to do, then God cannot be infinite and all powerful.

So as Muslims we try to do good. We leave the rest to Allah's mercy.

FARZANA K

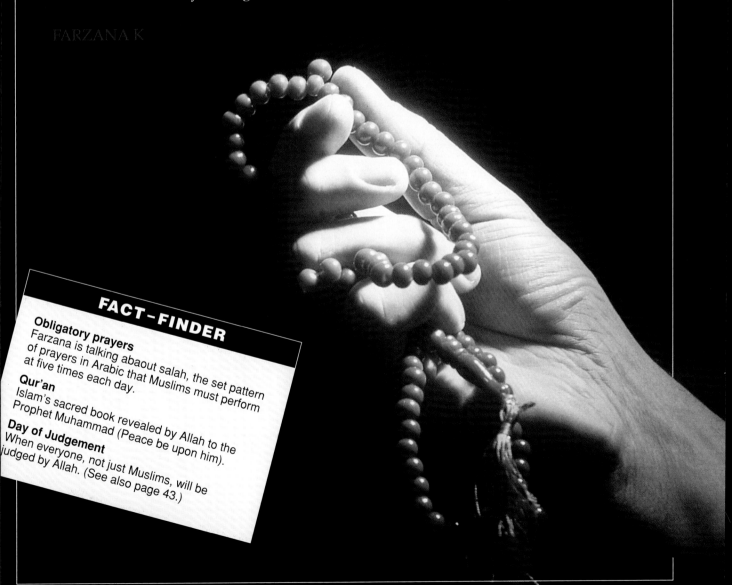

FACT-FINDER

Obligatory prayers
Farzana is talking abaout salah, the set pattern of prayers in Arabic that Muslims must perform at five times each day.

Qur'an
Islam's sacred book revealed by Allah to the Prophet Muhammad (Peace be upon him).

Day of Judgement
When everyone, not just Muslims, will be judged by Allah. (See also page 43.)

M y favourite words are 'peace', 'love' and 'harmony'. Those are the things that I really want in the world. At the moment, there's no love between quite a lot of countries, no peace, no harmony. In society, there's inequality, racism. The colour of your eyes or your skin shouldn't affect the way you're treated, but it does. People seem to think that just because you're coloured you're bad. It's not just whites doing that, it's blacks as well. You get blacks opposing Asians, Asians opposing whites, whites opposing blacks. It's a vicious circle, every sort of race opposing the other. Everywhere people are fighting each other.

I'd really, really like it if the whole world would come together and there was peace among everybody. But at least I can be peaceful myself – at home in the family, with my friends and in the community. I can avoid making enemies out of the people I live around and with. My mum, my brother, my dad, my relatives, my cousins, we haven't got a bad vibe between any of us. We're all caring towards each other. I want that to be an example to everybody in the world.

ANDLEEB S

THINGS I FIND CHALLENGING

The challenge for me is the future, really, because I don't really know what's ahead of me and I can't prepare for it. The only thing I can prepare for is the Day of Judgement. No-one knows when the Day of Judgement is going to come. At any moment, we could all find ourselves in front of Allah, answering for our actions, for what we've done. So I've got to be prepared for that every minute of my life. It means my whole life is a challenge.

When I think of the Day of Judgement, I think of myself standing in front of Allah with everybody else. All human beings are there, whatever their religion, and whether they have a religion or not. Each of us goes in front of Allah in turn and answers for our actions. When you are there in front of Allah, every part of your body speaks. If a thief goes in front of Allah, his hands speak for what he's stolen and his feet speak for taking him to the places where he stole things. You account for your actions, then God decides whether to place you in Heaven or in Hell.

I want to go to Heaven.

ANDLEEB S

2016
2015
2014
2013
2012
2011
2010
2009
2008
2007
2006
2005
2004
2003
2002
2001
2000
1

There are a lot of stereotypes about Muslim life, particularly about Muslim women. People say that Muslim women aren't allowed to do this, that or the other.

Islam restricts no-one. Islam regards the male and the female equally. Their physical characteristics aren't the same, but both have the same opportunities. Islam doesn't say that women can't go out or that they should be chained to the kitchen.

Islam says that a Muslim should study. We should aim to be at the top of our chosen field, and we should strive to the best of our ability. I see my studies as a form of worship. If I do well, I feel I am pleasing Allah. I've been given the gifts to study and I should utilize them. On the other hand, I don't want my studies to get in the way of my religious duties. If I have a big push on my studies, I feel am I worshipping my studies when I should be worshipping Allah, the Creator. It's a question of getting the balance right, but it isn't always easy.

At college, we are fortunate to have a prayer-room. Our tutors give us fifteen minutes for zuhr, the noon prayers. Basically, we just do the essentials then, which is four rak'ahs.

I have no problem with salah five times a day. Salah is compulsory, and we obey Islamic law just as everyone obeys the law of the land, like speed limits on the roads. In fact, when I pray it gives me a sense of relaxation, and that helps my studies. When I feel all tensed up, I just turn to God and pray, and I find it relaxes me. To me, salah is not a constraint, it's a gift.

IFZAL A

FACT-FINDER

Rak'ah
Sequence of set movements and set words repeated during salah two to four times, depending on the time of day.

Salah
Set pattern of prayers/worship that Muslims must perform at five times each day.

As I've told you, it was always my wish to go into further and higher education. I remember teaching my son Maths when he was preparing for his 11-plus. I'd left school so long before that I'd forgotten most of the things I'd learnt. I couldn't remember how to do fractions and was too embarrassed to ask anybody. Even simple exercises I couldn't do. So I went to the library and got some very basic books, pretending I was looking for some other purpose.

What I used to do was to go through the exercises before my son came home to make sure I could do them. I used to practise everything. Then, when he came in, I taught him.

I do find it challenging getting back into education, especially now that I'm doing it in a more serious way. Four years ago, I started studying properly – after fourteen years. I did GCSEs in Maths and English, then an Access course, and got a place at Westhill College, Birmingham.

I think the most challenging thing is finding the time. Time goes so fast. I don't have as much time as I need to get through the work. I have a house to clean, cooking to do, children to look after. I teach every evening at the mosque. I have so much to do. I do find it challenging. I find I can't study for as long as I could when I was younger. Still, I'm trying to achieve something.

MUSARAT S

FACT-FINDER

11-plus
Exam which he had to pass in order to get into a grammar-school. (See also page 35.)

I think the biggest challenge of living as a Muslim in this country is keeping to your faith, because there are many things to distract you. If you don't have a strong faith, you may be distracted. All the time, you have to keep in mind that you are a Muslim and there are certain things you cannot do, and certain things you must not do. Watching television presents quite a lot of difficulties. Some programmes contain things which to a Muslim are wrong: for instance, women not properly clothed. This is the kind of thing we have to be careful about.

However, because we live in a materialistic age, I would say that materialism is perhaps the greatest threat to any person of faith, whatever their faith may be. Part of the work of this Centre is to have a monthly meeting with our Christian friends. Materialism is one of the factors that we all tend to agree is damaging the moral basis of the society we live in.

MUHAMMAD AFZAL

FACT-FINDER

Materialistic
Dominated by the idea that material things are more important than anything else.

Moral
Morals are ideas or beliefs about what is right, what is wrong and how people should behave.

T rying to keep ourselves as Muslims with all the pressures of everyday life and being in a non-Muslim country – that's challenging.

FARZANA K

M uslims live in countries all over the world, places as different as India or China or Europe. They pick up some of the traditions and cultures and ways of life of local communities. Chinese Muslims, for instance, eat differently and dress differently. But what makes them Muslims is their belief in what is in the Qur'an and the traditions of the Prophet (Peace be upon him).

Islam sets boundaries for Muslims, and as long as we keep within them we can be with other people. When Muslims first went to Abyssinia – modern-day Ethiopia – there was a Christian king there. The Muslims asked the Prophet (Peace be upon him) how they should behave in a Christian kingdom. The Prophet said, 'Adopt what is good and leave what is bad.' I think that's what Muslims should be doing in Britain today. There are good things in this society and there are some bad things. Personally I think the good things are vanishing from this country and bad things are creeping in.

IBRAR K

FACT-FINDER

Qur'an
Islam's sacred book revealed by Allah to the Prophet Muhammad (Peace be upon him).

Prophet
Here, Muhammad, the final Prophet of Islam.

INDEX

Page numbers in **bold** type show where words or phrases are explained in FACT-FINDERS